THE ALL NEW STYLE OF MAGAZINE-BOOKS

SDMLIVE®

www.SDMLIVE.com

MP

MOCY PUBLISHING
WWW.MOCYPUBLISHING.COM

Printed by CreateSpace, An Amazon.com Company

TRBT
THE REAL BUSINESS TEAM

A MONTHLY SPOTLIGHT ON ENTREPRENEURS NATIONWIDE LISTED IN THE MOST EXCLUSIVE BUSINESS DIRECTORY.

WWW.THEREALBUSINESSTEAM.COM

SDM LIVE ®

EDITOR-IN-CHIEF
D. "Casino" Bailey
casino@sdmlive.com

EDITORIAL DIRECTOR
Sheree Cranford
sheree@sdmlive.com

GRAPHIC/WEB DESIGNER
D. "Casino" Bailey
casino@sdmlive.com

ACCOUNT EXECUTIVE
Katrina Carson
kartina@sdmlive.com

PHOTOGRAPHERS
Anterlon Terrell Fritz
Treagen Colston
Terance Drake

CONTRIBUTORS
Katrina Carson
No'el Snyder

COPY ORDERS & ADVERTISING OFFICE
Send Money Order or Check to:
Mocy Publishing
P.O. Box 35195
Detroit, Michigan 48235
(833) 736-5483
advertise@sdmlive.com

Copy Order Item
SDM Live Magazine Issue #21
S&H Plus Retail Price - $9.99 per copy

WWW.SDMLIVE.COM

Printed by CreateSpace, An Amazon.com Company

MP
MOCY PUBLISHING

ISSUE 21 - 2019
CONTENTS

pg. 12
TAZ BAILEY
Taking the rap battle scene to the mainstream with a new method.

pg. 16
SWIFTY & DUB
An all new beginning of how two men unite with acting & music.

pg. 20
DENNIS REED
New movie release "The First Lady".

pg. 23
TOP 10 CHARTS
The hottest albums and digital singles this month features Ella Mai, KFire Queen Naija and more.

1

**Rocketfish™ - 4-Port 4K HDMI
Switch Box - Black**
$79.99
www.bestbuy.com

2

**Logitech - Harmony Ultimate One
15-Device Universal Remote - Black**
$59.99
www.bestbuy.com

3

**Facebook - 10.1" Portal with
Alexa - Video Calling - White**
$199.99
www.bestbuy.com

LET'S TALK WITH

Katrina Carson

iHeart RADIO   SDM LIVE UNPLUGGED®

**TUNE IN AND LISTEN TO
LET'S TALK WITH KATRINA CARSON
EVERY MONDAY FROM 6PM - 7PM**
AS SHE GIVES YOU AN EXCLUSIVE
BACKSTAGE PASS TO THE LATEST
ENTERTAINMENT NEWS.

WWW.SDMLIVE.COM

Black is The New Color of Scandal

IS R. KELLY AND MICHAEL JACKSON BEING BLACKBALLED BY
THE MEDIA FOR THEIR ALLEGED SCANDALS WITH MINOR CHILDREN?

by Cheraee C.

Seems like every year one of our African American legends are under fire by the media and society. Lately, society has been targeting the late great Michael Jackson and R. Kelly. They're both being accused of engaging in inappropriate and unlawful sexual behaviors with minors. Their legacies are being tarnished as they lose revenue after revenue as a response to their alleged scandals.

Why does it seem like only African Americans are endlessly ridiculed by society? There are plenty of billionaires and millionaires from other cultures guilty of horrid scandals also, yet their scandals sit in silence. Yet they don't get media attention, they don't get jail time or face any type of criminal charges, and they don't get TV documentaries aimed to destroy their reputation and their character. The color of one's skin shouldn't be able to represent or identify how society depicts them when they become in trouble with law. Once you're famous, you may not be able to control being in the limelight, but one thing that should never change is equality.

THE HOTTEST RADIO SHOWS ON THE PLANET!

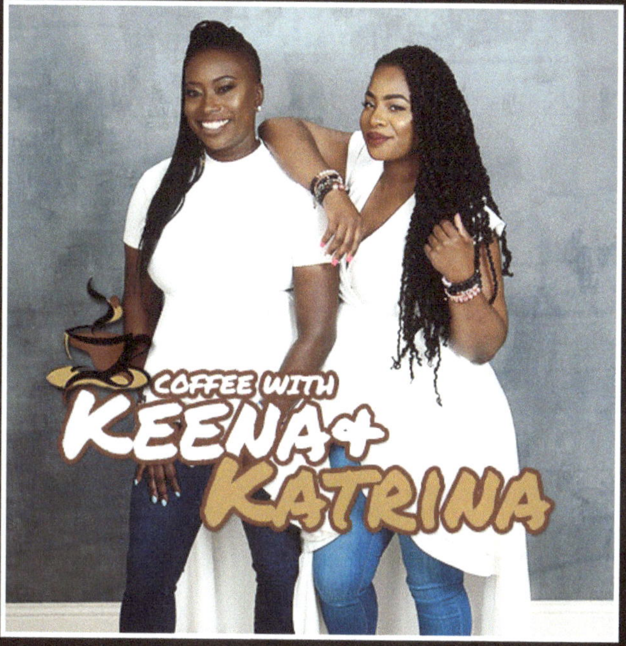

DOWNLOAD THE APPS

SDM Live, AnueYou Global Radio or iHeart Radio today!

Taz Bailey Ringside

MEDIA OF THE BATTLE RAP GAME TAZ BAILEY BUILDS HIS BRAND BY
BEING WELL RESPECTED IN THE GAME OF THE FINEST RAP STARZ.
by Katrina Carson

What is the bar structure?

The Bar Structure Is a Media Platform I created for
Battle Rappers, To Share Their Views & Opinions
On The Artform The Same Say Industry Can go
to Revolt, Breakfast Club Ect. And Also give my
analysis and breakdowns on Battles and certain
topics in the Battle Rap culture From the Perspec-
tive Of a HipHop Artist Who understands the
writing process of a Rapper.

What and who inspire you to construct/create a show centered around battle rap?

The Battlers themselves inspired me to creat the
show, as I spent countless hours in my small
apartment watching Battles for motivation for my
mixtape at the time and realize they don't have
many platforms where fans can get to know them
outside their battles. Also to cut out the confu-
sion of who wins each battle seeing that most of
them are not Judged and no official winner is ever
decided.

Do you feel that the bar structure will present battle rap to people in a different light? If so, why?

I think it will, depending on who's watching.
I have a lot of ppl that watch my show who are
unfamiliar with battle rap but Love HipHop, Also
A lot of Hardcore battle rap fans. I like to present
it to the ppl as a sort of Sport, and Hidden Genre
In Hip-Hop. That sports angle takes ppl out of the
mind frame of "These Guys Are So Disrespectful"
into the same mind state of a Boxing fans. It's a
War Of Words instead of fist which is how I like to
explain it.

When you think of the future of battle rap, 20/30 years from now, what do you see?

In 20/30 years Battle Rappers Will Have Better
Business And will be treated like athletes and
major artist with Various Sponsorships And
Brands wanted to have a piece in this currently
untapped market.

What other platforms are you planning to show the
bar structure in the future? BET, ESPN, REVOLT,
THISIS50

Do you feel as though battle rap is underrated in today society? If so, why and how?

No, Battle Rap is now being seen by millions and
Acknowledge by some of The Most Prestigious
Names And Brands In Our Culture. From Louis
Farrakhan Mentioning Loaded Lux In One His
Most recent speeches during his visit in Detroit,
Nick Cannon Hiring Top Tiers Battle Rappers as
the New Faces For Wilson Out (Conceited, sHitman
Holla, Charlie Clips, MyVerse) ESPN giving K-Shine
& DNA their own NFL Commercials, Floyd May-
weather Sponsoring The "Super Bowl Of Battle Rap"
Summer Madness 7 last summer, And Even Sprite
biting Smack's Slogan for their new Ad. Battle Rap is
alive and thriving.

The Man Making Changes

KEN DANDRIDGE IS A MAN OF INSPIRATION AS HE CONTINUES TO UTILIZE HIS PERSONAL EXPERIENCES TO MOTIVATE OTHER PEOPLE.

by Cheraee C.

Q. Tell us briefly about the name of your company and how it's name came along.

A. The name of our company Change Me was founded in Charlotte North Carolina. I was sitting in a library at one of the lowest points of my life. I had lost everything and my credit was in ruin. I had been going from job to job. After years of layoff and terminations I decided to change me. I began to seek out resources to help me out of my situation and I also began to study the credit industry after learning it was not very user friendly for the average consumer.

Q. What exactly is your company's mission and give us some examples of how you help assist your clients?

A. The company's mission is to seek out all the hurdles that a client may have in life and help them to overcome. Some of our clients may want to start a business, but they may have a suspended license, bad credit, or they may owe thousands in child support. We assist them with resolving all of these matters on issue at a time then we help them to start that new business as a result they are completely changed.

Q. How long has your company been in business and what makes your company so unique?

A. Change Me has been in business 11 years and we are a very unique company because we are tapping into the Detroit metro market that is very undeserved when it comes to the legal and financial matters. Our discounted pricing and our payment plans allow clients to be able to live today and clear up past matters.

Q. Describe one of your most memorable clients.

A. I have one client in mind that came to us. She needed our services rather urgently. She had been driving on a suspended driver's license for over 14 years and she owed over 8,000 in responsibility fees and tickets, and her DTE bill was over 5,000 dollars. Her reasoning for needing her license at the moment was that a non-profit group had selected her family to go on a all expense paid vacation with her and her four children to Disney World and her utilities were due to be shutoff. One of the requirements was that parent chaperones must be able to drive the 15 passenger van or no license no trip. Needless to say we were able to fully restore her driver's license in three weeks and her 5,000 DTE bill was now down to a 0 balance. She was able to take her family to Disney for a vacation that they will now remember for a lifetime.

Q. Tell us about your radio show and how you connected with the Anueyou Network?

A. How I came about Anueyou global Radio. One of my good friend/brother and co-worker Lee Scott came into the office one day and said he had a dream that I had a radio show. I literally laughed at him feeling that was very farfetched from my personality. He said were going to make it happen. I don't

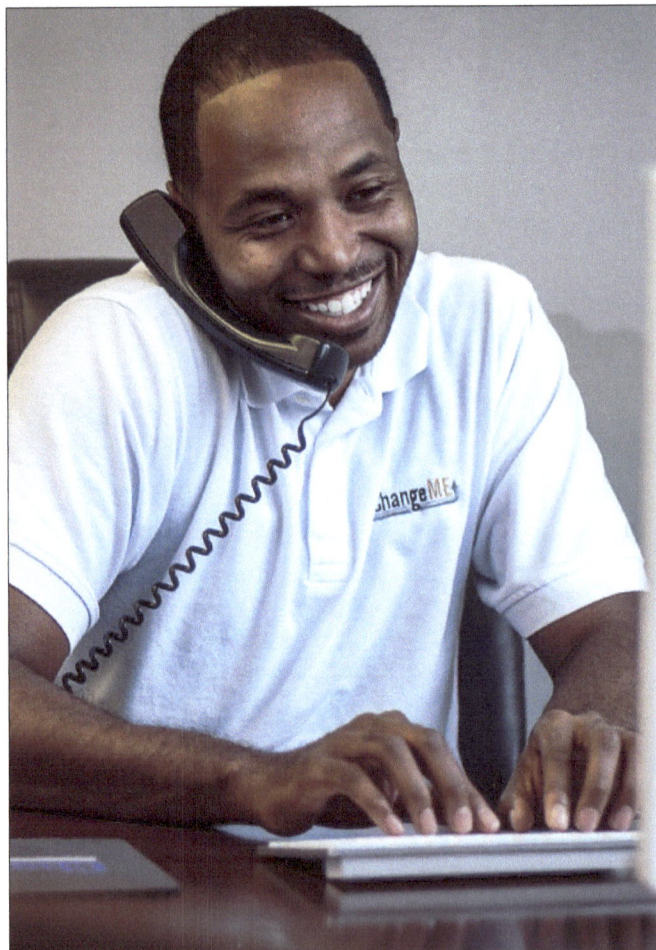

know how, but let's set up a photo shoot. We had a photographer Larry Web who was also a former player from Andover High School where Lee and I both coached basketball. The photo shoot went well with no idea of where to start with a talk show, I later was introduced to Attorney Shakeena Melbourne within two weeks of the initial discussion. After meeting with her she mentioned that she would be doing a radio broadcast and they looking for men to add to the show. It all started from here; I pondered on it and at one point said no to myself, but after reflecting on it for a few days I decided that this was ordained by God and I had a message to share with the world. So I moved on faith set an appointment with Katrina Carson and Casino and we met at a Starbucks. The first thing they asked for was photos and being that we already did the shoot it was a quick click of a button to send them. I was already prepared.

Q. How is your radio show doing thus far, and what have you learned being in radio?

A. Our following is picking up pretty fast only after about eight shows we started a clothing line and the best is yet to come. In the journey in radio which is uncharted territory for me, I have learned in life we can choose faith or we can choose fear, but when we choose faith on the other side of fear is greatness.

Coffee with Keena

KEENA IS A LAWYER AND A COMMUNITY ACTIVIST WHO IS FOCUSED ON BEING AN OUTLET FOR HER VENTURES AND SMALL BUSINESSES.

by Cheraee C.

Q. Tell us briefly about your radio show Coffee with Keena. What is your focus and who is your audience aimed at?

A. Coffee with Keena is a radio show about informing our community and providing necessary tools and resources in business development from experts in their specific fields. The focus of the show is small businesses. The audience is everyone. The radio show tailors to specific members of the community each month such as couples (married, engaged or dating), veterans, nutritional wellness, education and the like.

Q. So far to date, who had the most memorable interview you've done and what things did you enjoy about the interview?

A. The most memorable interview I have seen recently was Michelle Obama. She is currently on a book tour for her recent booked titled "Becoming Michelle Obama." I enjoyed Mrs. Obama's truth and her side of the story. Everyone from can see a point of view of an individual but no one truly understands the highs and lows of what it takes to get up each morning and take on a role, title or task. Some days are nerve-racking, built with insecurity and uncertainties. Other days are filled with spiritual uplifting, strength and full motivation. And I enjoyed the fact that Mrs. Obama shared all of these issues in her book and her interview.

Q. What inspired you to get into radio and how did you connect with the SDMLive Network?

A. I was inspired to get into radio by the mass media personnel, Casino Bailey. We engaged in a long conversation one evening as I shared my passion about helping veterans get re-socialized in society, because my brother is a veteran. We also discussed my passion of helping inform the community that there is hope. A lawyer should not be someone you just google but should be a great source for resources and tools to to help build and push your life forward. After this conversation, Mr. Bailey thought I would be great for radio. After 3 denial attempts, I was led to do a radio show and here I am 6 or more episodes later and have had listeners tune in from Jamaica, Canada, London, California and right here in Detroit, Michigan. I am just so grateful. Also, through Mr. Bailey's efforts, connections and networking I was able to connect with the SDMLive Network.

Q. What is your daily profession outside of hosting your own radio show?

A. My day job is an attorney. I am the principal attorney at Upton Law, PLLC, which is located at 24724 Farmbrook Road, Suite 100, Southfield, MI 48034. Our primary practice areas: business law, real estate law, estate planning (wills and trusts) and bankruptcy. We can be reached at www.uplawpllc.com or 248-677-6535.

Q. What led you to become a lawyer and start your own law firm?

A. I wanted to be a lawyer since I was about 5 years old. My mother likes to remind me about the times she caught me in my room talking to my teddy bears and cabbage patch dolls saying "I am the judge so explain your case." I do not know where that came from but I would have cases like Judge Judy with bears and dolls. Thereafter around the age of seven a teacher asked me what do I want to be when I grew up and I said a judge. She asked me to research and create a timeline of all of the education I needed to become a judge. I did just that and have been in tract my entire life.

Q. A lot of community leaders do volunteer work. Where do you volunteer at and what made you volunteer for these organizations?

A. I currently volunteer with the Center for Success, it is a literacy program in Detroit that helps students better their English skills, reading skills and build confidence in who they are through different programs and activities. I am a tutor/mentor for a little girl in 2nd grade and we just have a ball each weekly session getting to know each other and developing her skills. I also volunteer with Common Ground in Oakland County, where attorneys sit down with individuals in the community for 20-30 minutes to discuss future legal actions, pending legal disputes, discuss legal issues and concerns and fill out court documents and forms.

Storming the Movie Scene

BOTH PRODUCER DUBMUZIK AND RAPPER SWIFTY MCVAY GET INTIMATE ABOUT THE ROLES THEY PLAY IN A NEW DETROIT MOVIE TITLED DEVIL'S NIGHT.

by Cheraee C.

Dubmuzik

So Dubmuzik, what made you start producing music and who was the first artist you produced music for?

What made me start producing music was when my uncle DeWayne Holloway gave me my first turntable and mixer and all his records ever since then music has been my passion. The first artist I produced was with David McMurray of the Was not Was back in 1992, David McMurray was signed over on Warner Bros , David got me my first feature and placement when I was like 19yr of age.

How did you end up becoming the producer for the Devil's Night movie soundtrack?

The way that I ended up producing the devil's Night soundtrack was threw the homie Swifty McVay of D12, I worked with Swifty on the return of the dozen vol1 and 2 mixtape and the Gray Blood project. So when the chance came to work on the movie soundtrack me and my production partner Laidback was giving first dibs and we landed the placements on the Devil's Night movie soundtrack.

Is Devil's Night the first movie that you produced a soundtrack for? If not, what are some others?

Yes! Devil's Night is the first soundtrack I produced with many more to come in the near future.

In general would you rather produce soundtracks for movies or produce artist projects? Why or why not?

Both, why because I enjoy the music aspect of it all, being in the studio vibes, and the ability to create whatever I want is a win for me.

How did you go about selecting the music that was chosen to be a part of the soundtrack?

I was able to select the movie music by the simple vibe of the movie itself. Devil's Night!

What is your favorite single on the soundtrack and why?

My favorite single on the soundtrack is Phony, Why I picked this song is because the words go hand and hand with the story line being told in the move Devil's Night.

Outside of producing, what is your overall opinion of the upcoming film Devil's Night?

My overall opinion would be, I don't have one yet, reason being I haven't seen the move in its entirety as of yet but the trailer for the Devil's Night movie looks intriguing.

Swifty McVay

So Swifty, let's start by you letting us know how you got the opportunity to be apart of the upcoming film Devil's Night?

My son's karate instructor told me he was doing fight choreography for the movie. I suggested that it may be kind of dope if I submitted a song for the movie since my first D12 album was titled Devils Night. Also, I'm coming from a city that plays a part of that day before Halloween. He got the idea and connected me with the director of the movie and the rest was history

Can you give us a brief summary about what Devil's Night is mainly about and what inspired the name of the movie?

It's an action horror film about a urban legend monster that's terrorizing the city. Some believe in him and some don't!

What's the history behind the movie? Is it based on or inspired by a real life event or experience that took place in Detroit?

The Nain Rouge creature is something that's been talked about by Detroiters for years. They have parades based on it and everything.

What made you want to venture into acting and what was the first film you ever acted in?

I was asked by a movie director if I wanted to feature in a film in 2003 titled 7 Days in 7 Mile. When I accepted the role, I learned that not only did he have rehearsals, but he was having improv sessions every weekend that I was apart of to help me sharpen my skills and it was fun for me, I had a chance to meet some great people and it bought the acting bug out of me. My second film was The Longest Yard in 2005 with Adam Sandler, Burt Reynolds (R.I.P), and Chris Rock. By 2008 I was introduced to theatre which I really love and started doing plays so after that I knew acting is what I really wanted to do so I played in a couple more films, but Devils Night: Dawn Of The Nain Rouge was the first film I ever been in where I was on top on the movie soundtrack.

Besides yourself, what other notable actors and actresses will be featured in Devil's Night and which actor/actress did you enjoy working with the most on set?

I worked with a lot of dope local actors that's been doing their thing independently, Nathan Mathers (Eminem lil brother) is also in the film and I can say that I had fun working with EVERYONE on set. During this process, even the ones who worked behind the cameras were fun to work with and it was a dope experience.

Describe the role you play in the movie. What is your character's name, what type of persona do they have, can you personally relate to your character?

I'm playing the Mayor of Detroit and I'm hearing things about this urban legend, but at the same time I have other issues in my life I'm tending to. I'm not into politics in real life, but I'm glad I got that role cause it gave me a chance to let people see another side of me on screen they never saw other than a hip hop street guy, or gritty guy with a hamster persona.

When will the movie be released to the public and where will we be able to see it?

It will probably be released the spring of 2019 and the movie will be premiered at Emagine Theaters.

What is your overall opinion of the movie? Will there be a part 2 maybe? Do you plan to continue tackling more film projects?

I think the movie is dope and that my fans and non fans will really enjoy it. Haven't talked about a part two yet, but I continue to create more movies and do more auditions, and take the movie industry by storm in the future

New Deals, New Contracts Chris Brown Makes A Sweet Deal With RCA Records

by Cheraee C.

Chris Brown is walking into 2019 with a big game changer under his belt. Not only is he gearing up to release his sixth studio album with RCA Records, but he will become the youngest artist in history to own the master recordings to his music. RCA is very thrilled about the new deal and contract they have with Chris Brown. Hopefully, other artists will follow his footsteps and really start securing ownership of their music.

For those who don't know Chris Brown will be turning thirty this year and has been in the music industry since 2005. Never underestimate a young millionaire and how times are changing. Music labels are definitely going to have to step their game up from now on because artists are becoming more knowledgeable about the music business.

Making Power Moves

ENTREPRENEUR DENNIS REED DISCUSSES HIS MOTIVATION BEHIND
HIS LATEST MOVIE RELEASE THE FIRST LADY

by Cheraee C.

Q. Briefly tell us what led you to create your recently released movie The First Lady.

A. I reason I created the movie First Lady was simple - women, Women run the world honestly and they take on so much when their men can't step up for whatever reason that may be. I felt a woman boss would be the dopest thing ever.

Q. You had a lot of celebrities casted in your movie. Can you share who some of these celebrities are, and what they are most known for?

A. Well we had Jim Jones who is a rapper from New York. Then we had Nicole Alexander also known as Hoopz from the Flavor of Love. She is one of the most beautiful women in the world and we are not talking about her looks. Her whole personality is dope. We had Royce Reed from Basketball Wives. Royce is part of the family and been around for a minute.

Q. What led you to cast the actresses and actors that you chose to fit the roles in your movie?

A. Well I chose LeMastor Spragling because I don't make movies without him and velda Hunter. They are not only Dope but they are family and two of the best actors in the world. Demaris harvey was just a dude I kept seeing and he seem to just fit the roll and he murdered it. Julius Washington well let just say we were blessed to have him. He been in so many movies and tv shows. when he sent his tape in I knew he was the one. K Deezy man how can I put it? GOD the person who had the role quite on me 2 days before and dude got the script and murdered it. One of the dopest artist I know.

Q. Can you give us a brief storyline about the plot of The First Lady?

A. First lady is a movie about a woman who falls for a man that was the reason he man wasn't around in the first place.

Q. How long did it take you to actually film and edit this project and did you come across any roadblocks?

A. It took five months and the only road block was time. I wish we could have got the movie done faster.

Q. How can the viewers watch The First Lady and do you have more film projects on the way?

A. they can watch it on Amazon Prime, tubitv.com and Roku it will be in more places at the top of the year.

The Coldest Creator

FASHION DESIGNER AND BOUTIQUE OWNER KENYA IS KILLING THE
DETROIT SCENE WITH HER FASHION SHOWS AND ELITE FASHION PIECE.

by Cheraee C.

Q. What is the name of your boutique and what types of items do you sell?

A. The name of my boutique Is KOLD Kreationz Boutique! I sell ladies clothing, accessories and men bowties!

Q. What do you love about fashion and what does fashion mean to you?

A. Fashion is my LIFE! I have always been into it and I love everything about it. I get to travel and meet so many new people! I have always loved to dress and style others. Fashion is where I need to be.

Q.I know you do a lot of fashion shows so what was the most memorable fashion show you've done to date and why?

A. My most memorable runway show was this past June at The Roberts Riverwalk Hotel. I had over 50 models in Detroit & Surrounding Areas, My show sold-out & I had to add more chairs to accommodate my guests. We took so many nice pictures inside and on the river. The experience was AMAZING! Also I still get feedback from this event!

Q. If you could style any celebrity who would you style and why?

A. If I could style a celebrity I don't know off-hand who I would choose. I like to style people I know and work with. A possible person would be Michelle Obama or Oprah!

Q. How do you deal with all the stress, jealousy, sacrifices, and etc that come with being an entrepreneur?

A. There are so many things negative/positive that come with being an entrepreneur. I PRAY over my business daily to ensure and keep my sanity. I'm BLESSED to make it this far and

I have a long way to go. In January 2019, I will be celebrating five years in business and I'm so grateful. Thanks for your time and choosing me.

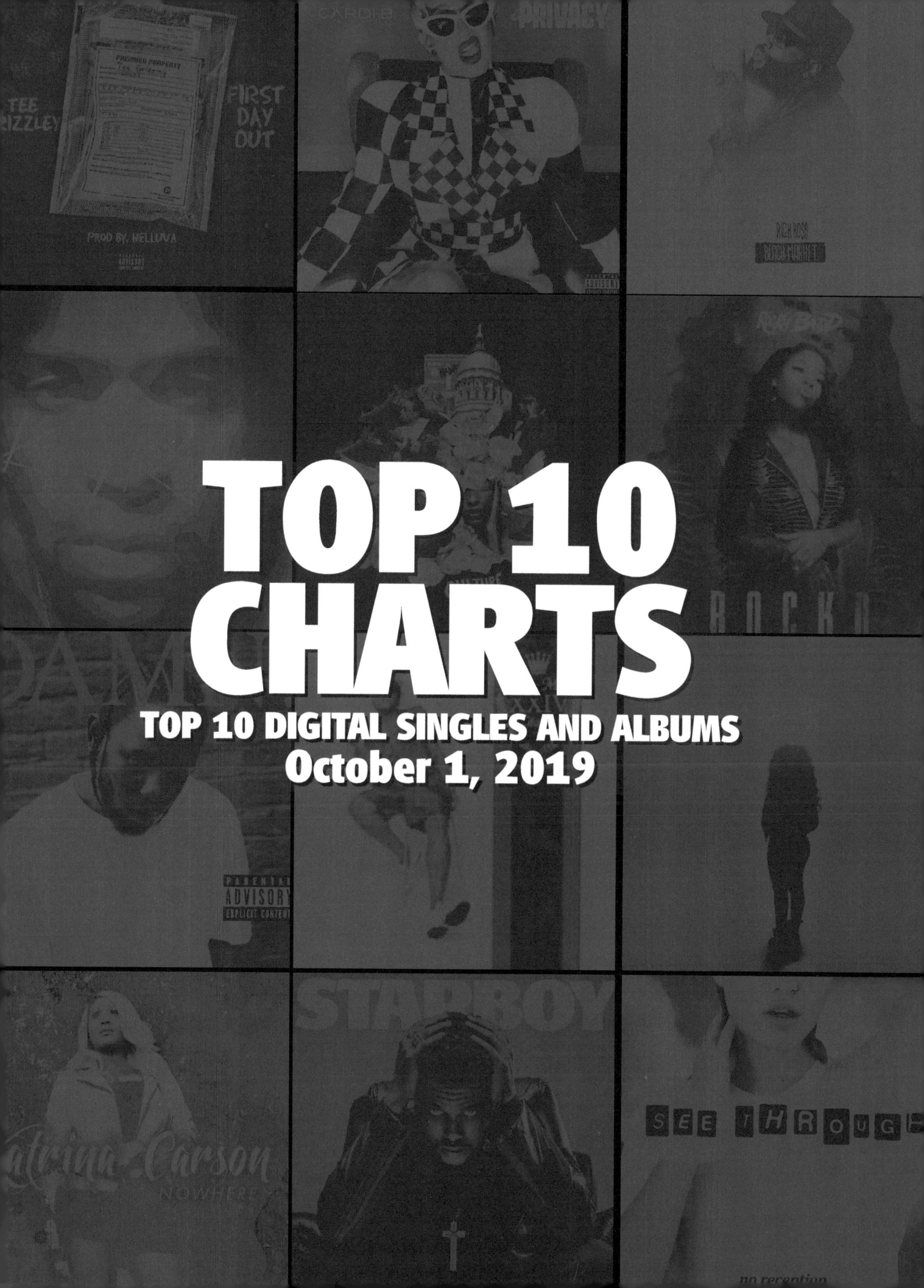

TOP 10 CHARTS

TOP 10 DIGITAL SINGLES AND ALBUMS
October 1, 2019

ELLA MAI PERFORMING LIVE WITH HER HIT SINGLE "BOO'D UP" AND "TRIP" ON "SNL".

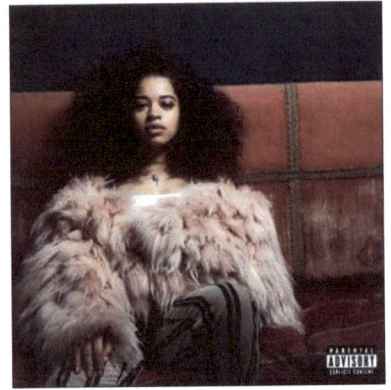

Ella Mai
Ella Mai

An R&B sensation Ella Mai drops a new self-titled ablum filled with hits excutive produced by Dj Mustard.

TOP 10 SINGLES
CHART OF THE MONTH

No.	Artist - Song Title
1	ELLA MAI - TRIP
2	CARDI B - MONEY
3	TYGA - TASTE
4	KATRINA CARSON - NOWHERE
5	DRAKE - NON STOP
6	KING DILLON - SUPER DRIP
7	LIL WAYNE - UPROAR
8	LIL DUVAL - SMILE FT. SNOOP DOGG AND BALL GREEZY
9	YELLA BEZZY - THAT'S ON ME
10	DION PRICE - NOVACANE

TOP 10 ALBUMS
CHART OF THE MONTH

No.	Artist - Album Title
1	ELLA MAI - ELLA MAI
2	LIL WAYNE - THA CARTER III
3	QUEEN NAIJA - QUEEN NAIJA
4	KING DILLON - THIRTY-ONE-THREE
5	NIKKI MINAJ - QUEEN
6	DRAKE - SCORPION
7	CARDI B - INVASION OF PRIVACY
8	DION PRICE - HEART OF A LION
9	MIGOS - CULTURE II
10	H.E.R. - H.E.R.

Horns & Halos
ARTIST: KFIRE
RATING: 5

Horns and Halos introduces the battling theme of good and evil/angels versus demons as the young music artist locates balance, after allowing christ to enter her life. Within the Detroit artist lyrics, K. Fire struggles with her family not believing in her goals, which results in the repercussions of her seeking approval through the different types of males she's encounted. As society hurdles negativity, K. Fire stumbles upon the situations that were never resolved within herself. Now she's focused on her faults and making her weaknesses her strengths. The varied, production was mostly done by Throne Muzik, with additional production from Ravo, and Verbatum. These instrumentals were fully compelling, powerful, and enjoyably solid. One of the tracks that stood out to my ears was titled Grateful. This track urges us to have a spirit of gratitude, with appreciation of it all no matter the negative or positive. This track also offers assistance in reflection on what God has done for ones life. With soulful features from Gerard Brooks and Paris Simone that set the tone for the album and an amazing verse from Lance Hitch on the track titled, Crown, K. Fire's delivery was extremely eloquent, which gave a confident approach towards all ten tracks, making this LP a classic hip-hop album with it being structured so well. The absolute best part about Horns and Halos was that there wasn't a single usuage of profanity within her lyrics, and that's truly a rarity in the music genre of hip-hop. Be sure to check out K. Fire's debut album Horns and Halos on ITunes, Google Play, and Spotify. Links provided below.

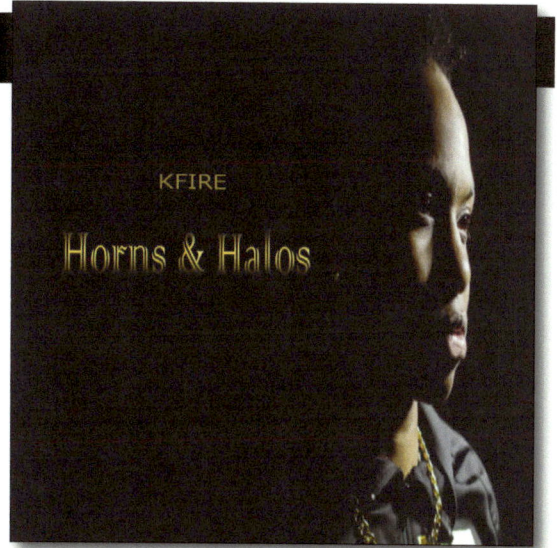

See Through
ARTIST: No Reception
RATING: 4

I've been invested in the music genre of hip-hop over these past few months, but recently, I acquired a punk/rock music project that provided delicate vocals of strength, alongside raging lyrics of appreciation. No Reception graces us listeners with her one woman, punk rock EP, See Through.

The nineteen-year-old songwriter sonically lures us music lovers into the subconscious mind of an artist whose self-reflection outshines the production on this four-track EP. Doing a hundred percent of the instrument playing and songwriting, we listeners obtain a glimpse into the woman behind these soothing, chaotic vocals. No Reception provides transparent lyrics that are strongly dedicated to her loved ones, who, on any occasion, she was unconditionally present for, but as the time approached for them to reciprocate the similar benefits of support and love, they proved unable. This provoked No Receptions' decision to isolate herself from the people who've taken advantage of her love and kindness, as she buries herself into "do not disturb" mode throughout See Through. The talented New York native greatly integrates thrash, melodic singing, subtle percussive guitar strings, and bass, with subversive drum strikes to the cymbals we hear throughout this short collection of tracks. Songs such as Door Mat and Can't Be Fixed supply an aggressive, thunderous rhythm, rendering a strong affirmation towards the lyrics. The track Losing Myself To You offers a pleasant guitar melody that provides a blissful intermix with her shrieking vocals, making this track a fan favorite for a strong sensation of solace with a calming release. No Reception delivers a star-studded performance that awards consistency and conviction for her vengeful, pulsating lyrics. Check out No Reception's debut EP, See Through on all digital streaming services, and also check out the visuals for no receptions. single, Time To Kill via YouTube. Links provided below.

HEELS &
SKILLZ

Nona Malone
is a beautiful model
from Houston, TX.

instagram
@nonamalone313

Photography by
@barearmy

Gaggy Sky

A sexy model
from Detroit MI.

instagram
@missgabbysky

HEELS &
SKILLZ

Photography by
@barearmy

HEELS & SKILLZ

Kendra Kouture

A video and runway model from Muskegon, MI.

instagram
@kouture_world

Photography by **@barearmy**

Cheraee's Corner
WHY CAN'T PEOPLE KEEP THEIR RELATIONSHIPS PRIVATE?

by Cheraee C.

Everything is not meant for the internet especially relationships as people makeup and breakup every day. It's nothing wrong with being real or open, but keep your love life private. Celebrities and non-celebrities manage to keep a lot of things private so it's no excuse to disclosing your relationship. People only know what you allow them to know, so keep people out of your business. Even the securest relationships have to be protected because people, society, etc will do whatever it takes to destroy your happiness. Temptation is everywhere, homewreckers, sidepieces, mistresses, etc are waiting for new opportunities.

Keep your relationship flaunting and showboating to a minimum. Don't awaken someone else's jealous, deceptive, lustful ways. People love wanting things and people that they cannot have. Don't think your ever to good to get played so always be mindful, and be private.

NEXT 2 BLOW

PISTOL P

Q. What's your goal for your music career in 2019?
A. My goal for 2019 is really just exposure so I can make a name for myself to get people to know me and who I am as well as my music. I want people to really see the passion for what I do. This is my form of art. It brings out a different side of me.

Q. What are three things you would like your fans to know about you?
A. I'm very well-reserved, silly, and I'm down to earth so that allows me to show respect to everyone.

Q. What do you enjoy most about performing?
A. I love the adrenaline rush I get every time and I'm starting to get addicted to it.

Q. If you could sign to any record label right now who would you sign to and why?
A. If I could sign to any label my first choice would definitely be Quality Control (QC) because so far I haven't seen or heard any bad reviews from them and all of their artists are making major moves right now in the music industry.

Q. Who are three of your favorite mainstream artists right now and three of your favorite underground artists?
A. My favorite mainstream artists include Young Jeezy, Chris Brown, Joyner Lucas, and underground artists include King Dillion, MoneyMakinMirr, and Sada Baby.

Q.

Q. As an artist how do you feel about all this hype that Jaquees is the king of R&B?

A. If that's how he feel then I can't argue with that, I was always told to believe in yourself. He definitely started controversy, and people talking about it. He put himself in the news so that was a smart move in my book!

Q How did you manage to drop a single on Empire for distribution?

A.My manager set me up with the right people who seen potential in me, so it was only right!

Q. What single did you drop and how do you feel like that power move has benefited your music career?

A. The single is titled "No Tic Toc." It let people know that I have a great flow, delivery, and I'm real because people can relate to it (No time for B.S)

Q. What are some of your views on distribution as an artist?

A. I think it's important because without it you will be limited on promotion. You want to attack every platform and reach out to the masses!

Q. What can your fans expect from T Tha Great in 2019?

A. Expect growth, progress, truth, knowledge, motivation. I'm not your typical rapper lol. I talk motivation through my music, I talk loving yourself and not worrying about what people think about you through my music. You can also expect performances, more visuals, and maybe a tour or two....So basically expect for me to extend my ladder and climb to the top!

NEXT 2 BLOW

T THA GREAT

SNAP SHOTS

Email Your Snap Shots to
snapshots@sdmlive.com

Urban Fiction, Spiritual, Motivation and more.
Order a book from Mocy Publishing today and receive FREE shipping.

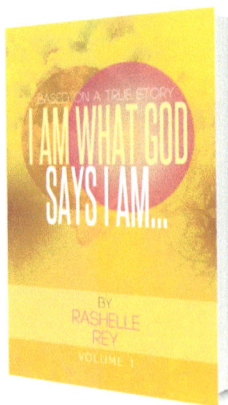

I Am What God Says I Am...
By Rashelle Rey

Item #: IAWGS29
Price: $9.99

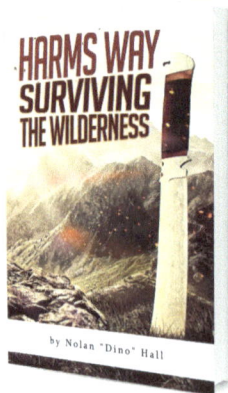

Harm's Way
By Nolan "Dino" Hall

Item #: HWS821
Price: $15.99

The Shadiest Mission Ever
By Cheraee C.

Item #: TSME28
Price: $12.99

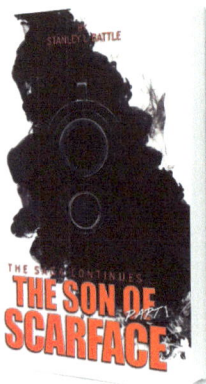

The Son Of Scarface – Part 1
By Stanley L. Battle

Item #: TSOS01
Price: $12.99

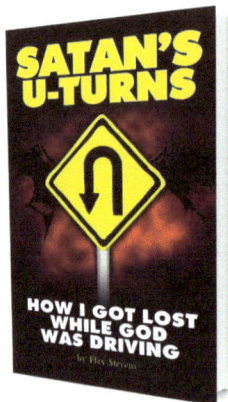

Satan's U-Turns
By Flex Stevens

Item #: SUT382
Price: $9.99

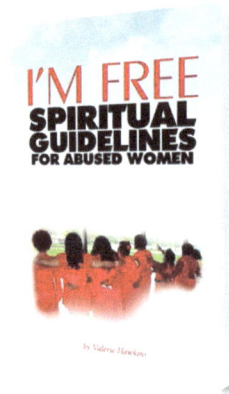

I'm Free
By Valerie Hawkins

Item #: IFTSG82
Price: $14.99

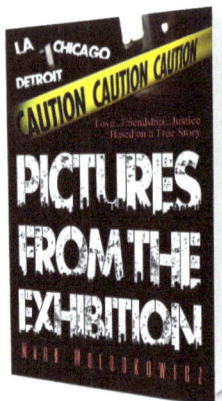

Pictures From The Exhibition
By Mark Wolodkowicz

Item #: PFAE292
Price: $15.99

Behind The Scenes
By Pamela Marshall

Item #: BTS721
Price: $15.99

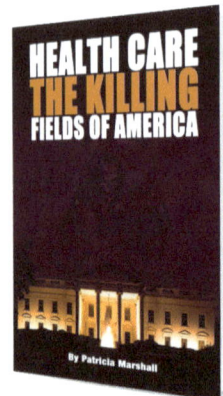

Health Care
By Patricia Marshall

Item #: HCTABF2
Price: $17.99

www.mocypublishing.com
order online and receive FREE shipping. Limit time offer.

THE ALL NEW STYLE OF MAGAZINE-BOOKS

www.ingramcontent.com/pod-product-compliance
Lightning Source LLC
Chambersburg PA
CBHW040036050426
42452CB00026B/39